THE SACRED TREE

Dedicated to the countless clans, tribes and nations of indigenous people throughout Mother Earth whose sacred visions, dreams, prayers, songs, wisdom, experience and kind guidance form the foundation and living reality of the *Sacred Tree*.

Original *Sacred Tree*
Produced Collaboratively by:
Judie Bopp
Michael Bopp
Lee Brown
Phil Lane

Adapted for Easy Reading by:
Judie Bopp
Michael Bopp
Phil Lane
Carolyn Peter

Illustrations by:
Patricia Morris

Technical Support:
Barbara Dudley
Mary Berg
Charlotte Gilbert

Produced by:
The Four Worlds Development Project
The University of Lethbridge
Lethbridge, Alberta
Canada, T1K 3M4

Project Coordinator:
Phil Lane, Jr.

April 1988

Funding provided by:
National Native Alcohol and Drug Abuse
Program of Health and Welfare Canada

**This Special Edition is adapted for
approximately a grade eight reading level.**

Four Worlds Development Project
The University of Lethbridge
4401 University Drive
Lethbridge, Alberta
T1K 3M4

ISBN #0-919555-54-3

The Four Worlds Development Project is the result of many people's efforts and wisdom. Some were directly involved, while others inspired us through their work in the fields of education, human and community development, health promotion and substance abuse.

Direction for this project was first set at a historic council held in Lethbridge, Alberta in December, 1982. Participants at the council were Native elders, cultural leaders and professionals from various communities across North America who gathered to address the root causes of Native alcohol and drug abuse. It was this gathering that gave birth to the Four Worlds Development Project.

In February of 1987, many of the elders and cultural leaders who participated in the original council, reinforced by others (over 100 in all) representing some 40 tribes from across North America, gathered at St. Paul's Treatment Centre on the Blood Reserve near Cardston, Alberta. They were invited to review the philosophy, guiding principles, activities, and strategies for human and community development articulated and implemented by the Four Worlds Development Project during its first four years, and to give direction and guidance for the years to come.

The elders and their collaborators were overwhelming in the strength of their support, approval and encouragement for all aspects of the Four Worlds Development Project. We are therefore confident in saying that the philosophy and principles the Project is based upon, as well as the processes, strategies, activities and vision of the future outlined in these documents, have received the full and unreserved support of the many respected Native elders and cultural leaders from across North America who attended this historic council.

The contribution of these dedicated leaders was framed by their own commitment to Native people and their own, often hard won, experience. To each of them we offer our deepest respect and appreciation. It is with their continued encouragement, guidance and prayers that we proceed "toward the year 2000" with the complete faith that Mother Earth and all her people will be healed.

In Recognition

In appreciation for their encouragement, wisdom, and guidance, we list here the names of those Native cultural leaders and their collaborators who participated in the two historic councils which gave birth and direction to the Four Worlds Development Project.

GARRY ABBOTT
DR. CRUZ ACEVEDO, Jr.
MARY ANDERSON
JOAN ARLEE
WALTER AUSTIN
SAM BALD EAGLE AUGUSTINE
LISE BASTIEN
HAROLD BELMONT
MARK BELMONT
ERNEST BENEDICT
MARY BERG
ANDY BLACK WATER
GARY BONNEAU
DR. MICHAEL BOPP
JUDIE BOPP
MAY BOTTLE
LEE BROWN
JOE BUGGINS
MRS. JOE BUGGINS
TOMMY BURNSTICK
ED CALF ROBE
ART CALLING LAST
CHIEF ANDY CHELSEA
MYRNA CHIEF STICK
CHIEF HARRY CHONKOLAY Sr.
WILLIAM COMMANDA
ANNIE COTTON
STEVE COURCHENE
RICHARD CRAFT
JOE CROWSHOE
JACKIE CRYING HEAD
HARRY DAHDONA
RICKI DEVLIN
JEANNIE DICK
CATHI DUPUIS-SHORTMAN
TYRONE EAGLE BEAR
GREGG ERICKSON
PERRY FONTAINE
ED FRED

DAWN FRY
NAPOLEON GARDINER
LEONARD GEORGE
CINDY GINNISH
BEATRICE GOOD STRIKER
GEORGE GOOD STRIKER
RUFUS GOOD STRIKER
WOODROW GOOD STRIKER
CATHIE GOTTFRIEDSON
LAURA HARRY
BLAIR HARVEY
ELIZABETH K. HAWKINS
CHRISTINE HAWTREE
ADELAIDE HEAVY SHIELDS
ED HEAVY SHIELDS
DR. PETER HEFFERNAN
ELAINE IGNATIUS
GAIL IRANI
ANTONIA JACK
CHICO JACK
HAROLD JACK STARR
HENRY D. JOHNSON
PHILLIP JOHNSON
JOE L. JOJOLA
BILLY JOSEPH
MICH KABAY
KATHY KING
GERMAINE KINUNWA
LIONEL KINUNWA
BOW LANE
PHIL LANE, Sr.
PHIL LANE, Jr.
YVAN LEBEL
ALBERT LIGHTNING
EVELYN LOCKER
ARVOL LOOKING HORSE
PHIL LUCAS
JOHN MANY CHIEFS
SANDY MANY CHIEFS

MARGARET MANY FINGERS
EVELYN MARTINE
JOANNE MERCREDI
LORNIE METCHOOYCAH
JON METRIC
JEFFREY MORIN
GREG MULHAIR
ALLAN MURRAY
PAUL NARCISSE
ELIZABETH NYMAN
WILSON OKEYMAW
DON PETER
LEE PIPER
ALDEN POMPANA
DAVID POWLESS
BOB ROACH
DOREEN RABBIT
DR. CHUCK ROSS
DR. ITA ROZENTAL
DR. MANUEL ROZENTAL
JERRY SADDLEBACK
HERMAN SAULIS
HARRY SHADE
MARIE SHUTER
ADELINE M. SINGER
ALEX SKEED
ART SKENANDORE
DR. FRANK SOVKA
LILLIE SQUIOUINHAN
ANGELINE STANDING ALONE
DOREEN STERLING
MARGE ST. EVENS
ERIC TOOTOOSIS
BERNICE VASS
KITTY WADSWORTH
MIKE WHITE
GILBERT W. WHITE DUCK
ROSE YELLOW FEET
KATHLEEN YOUNG PINE

Editorial Note:

In English it is impossible to refer to a person without using a pronoun that indicates gender or sex (e.g. he or she, him or her, his or hers). Since there is no special word to refer to a person whose gender is not know, most writers have chosen to use the masculine form in these situations.

This custom of using the masculine form when referring to a person whose gender is not known to be female, has caused a conspicuous absence of reference to women in English writing.

Thus all of the great ideas and discoveries discussed in English literature are expressed in masculine terms and the reader constantly visualizes males, rather than females, as active participatants in the world. Our society's tendency to devalue the role and contributions of women is only augmented by this lack of picturing women in an active, creative role.

The Four Worlds Development Project has chosen to alternate the use of feminine and masculine pronouns whenever the reference is unspecific. This choice of usage is a deliberate one to avoid the awkwardness of the compound form (he/she; him or her) while at the same time acknowledging the harmful consequences of bowing to a convention that persistently forces its audiences to visualize the world as dominated by men and operating on ideas expressed in masculine terms.

Table of Contents

"Then I was standing on the highest mountain of them all, and round about beneath me was the whole hoop of the world. And while I stood there I saw more than I can tell and I understood more than I saw; for I was seeing in a sacred manner the shapes of all things in the spirit, and the shape of all shapes as they must live together like one being. And I saw that the sacred hoop of my people was one of many hoops that made one circle, wide as daylight and as starlight, and in the center grew one mighty flowering tree to shelter all the children of one mother and one father. And I saw that it was holy."

Black Elk

(*Black Elk Speaks*, as told through John G. Neihardt, University of Nebraska Press, Lincoln, 1961)

I. THE STORY OF THE SACRED TREE

For all the people of the earth, the Creator has planted a *Sacred Tree* under which they may gather. This is where people find healing, power, wisdom and safety. The roots of this tree spread deep into the body of Mother Earth. Its branches reach up like hands praying to Father Sky. The fruits of this tree are the good things the Creator has given to the people: love, caring for others, generosity, patience, wisdom, fairness, courage, justice, respect, humility, and many other wonderful gifts.

The elders taught us that the life of the Tree is the life of the people. If the people wander too far away from the safety of the Tree, if they forget to eat its fruit, or if they should turn against the Tree and try to destroy it, great sadness will fall upon the people. Many will become sick at heart. The people will lose their power. They will stop dreaming dreams and seeing visions. They will begin to argue among themselves over little things. They will no longer be able to tell the truth, or be honest with each other. They will forget how to live in their own land. Their lives will become filled with anger and sadness. Little by little they will poison themselves and everything they touch.

Those who have gone before us said these things would happen, but they also said that the Tree would never die. And as long as the Tree lives, the people will live. It was said that the day will come when the people will wake up, as if from a long, drugged sleep: that they will begin to search again for the *Sacred Tree*. They will be timid at first, but little by little, they will understand how important this search is.

The location of the Tree and its fruits have been carefully guarded and preserved in the minds and hearts of wise elders and leaders. These humble and loving souls will guide anyone who is honestly and sincerely looking for the path leading to the protecting shadow and fruits of the *Sacred Tree*.

II.   IMPORTANT CONCEPTS

Symbols

A Symbol is anything human beings use to express or represent ideas and feelings that are important to them.   Symbols represent meaning. Sometimes a whole set of ideas and feelings can be represented by one symbol. Meaning helps human beings to gain purpose and understanding in their lives. If we live without symbols, we live without the full meaning of life. Ways of showing meaning through symbols include the symbol systems of mathematics, spoken and written language and the arts often meaningful dreams about ourselves and our lives also use symbols.

The Medicine Wheel

This is an ancient symbol used by almost all the Native people of North and South America. There are many different ways that this symbol is used: the four grandfathers, the four winds, the four directions, the four stages of life and many other things that can be talked about in sets of four. Just like a mirror can be used to see things not normally seen (like behind us, or around a corner), the medicine wheel can be used to help us see or understand things we can't quite see or understand because they are ideas and not physical objects.

11

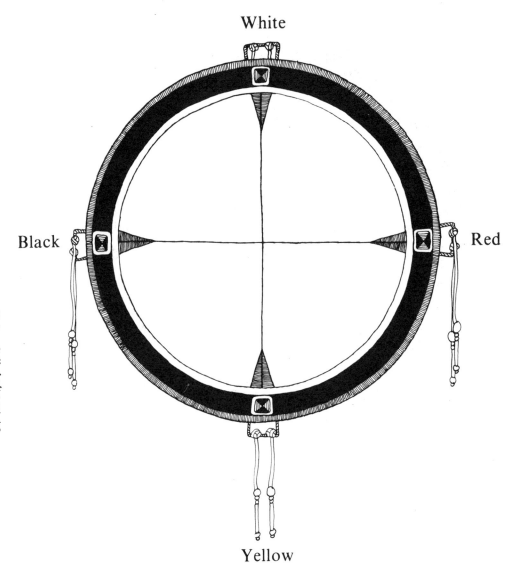

White

Black

Red

Yellow

The Medicine Wheel

We can think of the human family as having four symbolic races; red, yellow, white and black. The medicine wheel teaches us that the four symbolic races are all part of the same human family. All are brothers and sisters living on the same Mother Earth.

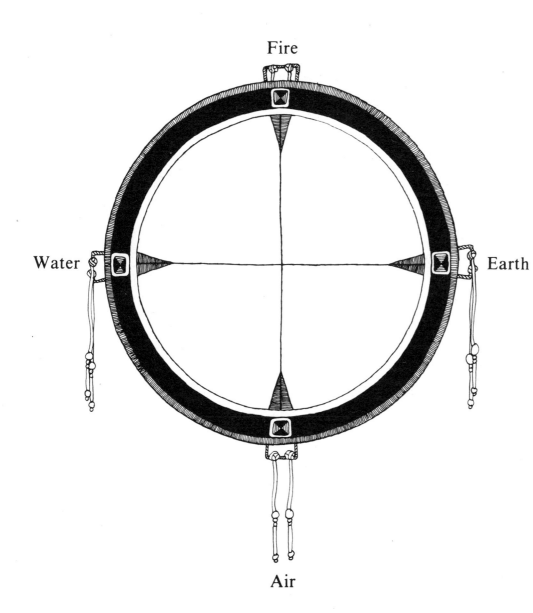

Fire

Water

Earth

Air

The Medicine Wheel

The medicine wheel teaches us that the four elements, earth, air, fire and water, are all part of the same physical world. All must be respected equally for their gift of life.

13

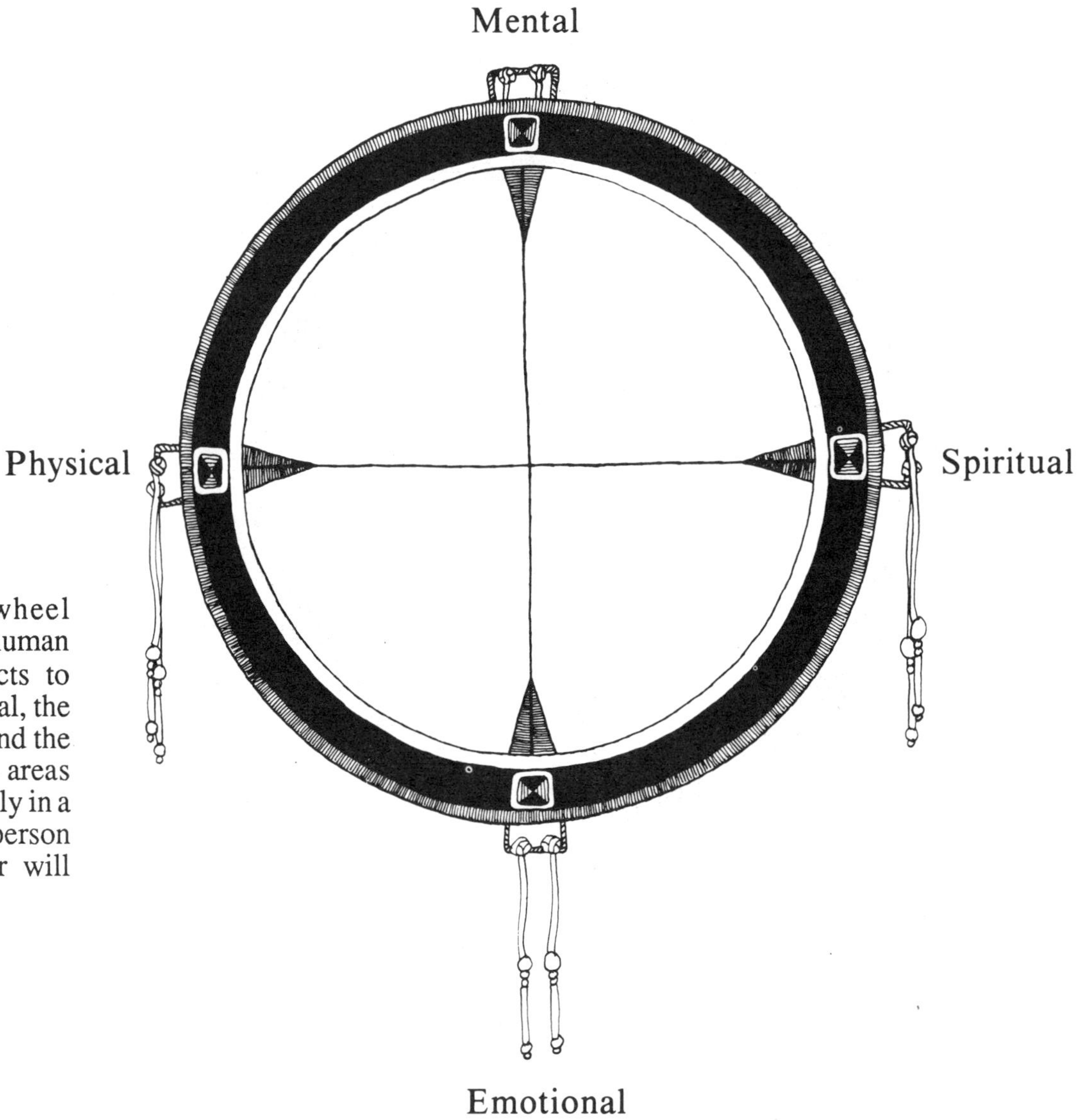

Mental

Physical

Spiritual

The Medicine Wheel

The medicine wheel teaches us that human beings have four aspects to their natures: the physical, the mental, the emotional, and the spiritual. Each of these areas must be developed equally in a healthy, well-balanced person through the use of our will power.

Emotional

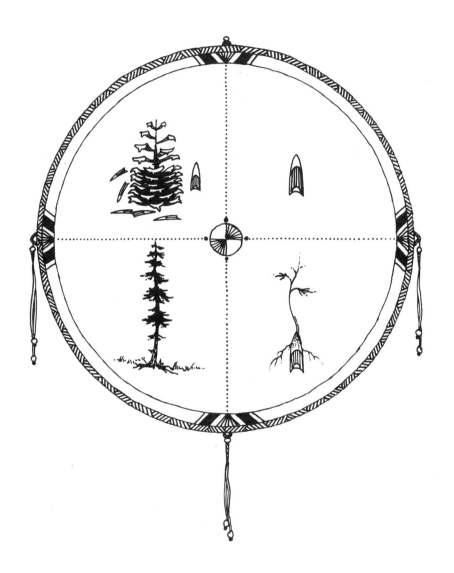

Potential

A seed has the potential to grow into a tree. The four aspects of our nature (the physical, the mental, the emotional and the spiritual) are like seeds. Each aspect has the potential to grow into powerful gifts.

Volition

Volition is another word for "will". We can use our volition (our willpower) to help us develop the many aspects of our nature. Volition is the force that helps us make decisions and then act to carry out those decisions. We can learn to use our volition by carrying out each of its five steps:

1. attention or concentration
2. goal setting
3. taking action
4. sticking to the action (not giving up)
5. finishing the action

Since volition is a primary force in developing all of our human potential, it is placed at the center of the medicine wheel.

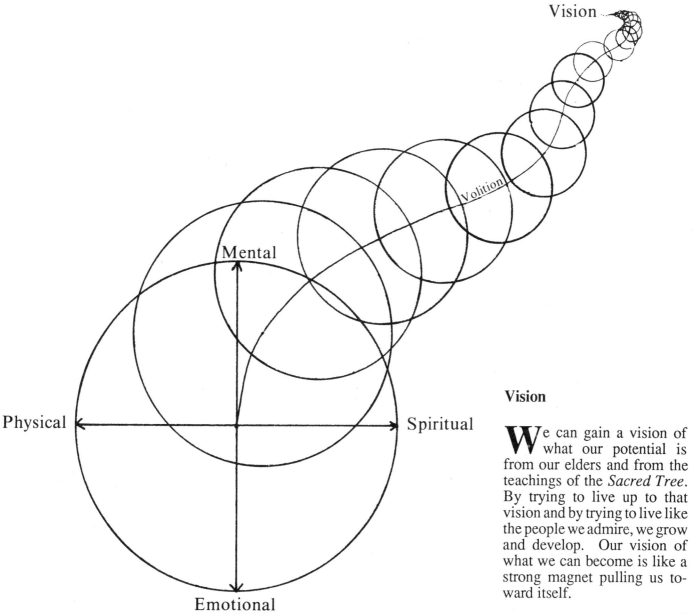

Vision · · · ·
Volition
Mental
Physical ← → Spiritual
Emotional

Vision

We can gain a vision of what our potential is from our elders and from the teachings of the *Sacred Tree*. By trying to live up to that vision and by trying to live like the people we admire, we grow and develop. Our vision of what we can become is like a strong magnet pulling us toward itself.

Growth and Change

All human beings have the capacity to grow and change. All of our hidden gifts can be developed when we have a vision of what is possible, and when we use our volition (will) to change our actions and our way of thinking. Little by little we can grow to our vision of a happy, healthy human being.

Identity

A person's identity consists of:

Body awareness: how you experience your physical presence

Self-concept: what you think about yourself and your potential

Self-esteem: how you feel about yourself and your ability to grow and change

Self-image: how you see yourself

Self-determination: your ability to use your volition (will) to develop your physical, mental, emotional and spiritual potential

19

Values

To value something means to care about it. We can get clues about what people value, when we watch what they do. The way people use their energy tells us about what they think is important.

If there is not a balance between what we value for ourselves and what we valued for others, we will not be able to keep developing our potential. This is because our own development is connected to the condition of the people around us. There are good values and bad values. If we only care about ourselves, even when it hurts others, the people around us will suffer. In the end, their hurt will become our hurt. It is important to value (to care for) ourselves. It is also important to care for others. These two values, self and others, must be kept in balance. If they are not, individuals, families, and even whole communities suffer and die. To be out of balance is to be diseased.

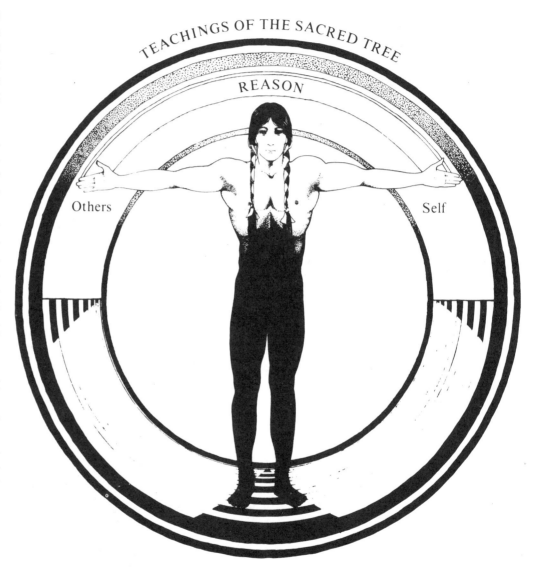

21

III. THE SYMBOLIC TEACHINGS OF THE SACRED TREE

Introduction

The *Sacred Tree* is a symbol. Symbols express meaning, and meaning helps us to find direction and understanding in our lives. The first people put symbols on the walls of caves. Since then, symbols have preserved much of what we have learned. They have even guided us into outer space. Perhaps the most important use of symbols is that they can help us to understand the deeper meanings of life.

In order to be in balance within ourselves, and with our family and community, we must find meaning, purpose and direction in life. Without meaning, purpose and direction, human beings become sick. We can measure the health and positive creative energies in a community by looking at the symbols the people use and how they live out their belief in these symbols. If we live without symbols, we will not be able to grow and develop to our full potential. Each time that people begin to strive to live according to the teachings of the *Sacred Tree*, they will begin to heal themselves and to come alive again.

The Symbol of the Sacred Tree

The *Sacred Tree* is a very important symbol for the Native people of the earth. For as far back as people can remember, it has given meaning and hope to many tribes and nations. As a symbol, the *Sacred Tree* has helped people organize their beliefs, their lives, their religions and their nations. It is a very deep symbol, with enough meaning in it to think about for a lifetime.

The *Sacred Tree* represents life, cycles of time, the earth, and the universe. The meaning of the *Sacred Tree* is linked to the medicine wheel. The centre of the medicine wheel is a symbol for the centre of the tribe and of creation. The *Sacred Tree* is also placed at the centre of the tribe. We can see this when we listen to the song about the *Sacred Tree* which is part of the sun dance.

> *I am standing*
> *In a sacred way*
> *At the earth's center*
> *Beheld by the people*
> *Seeing the tribe*
> *Gathered around me. (Lamedeer)*

(*Seeker of Visions*, by John Fire Lamedeer and Richard Eros, Simon and Schuster, New York, 1972, p. 205.)

The Four Great Meanings of the Sacred Tree

The four meanings of the *Sacred Tree* can be shown on the four points of the medicine wheel. In this way we can see them as parts of the cycle of human development as we grow from birth toward unity with the wholeness of creation. The four great meanings of the *Sacred Tree* are:

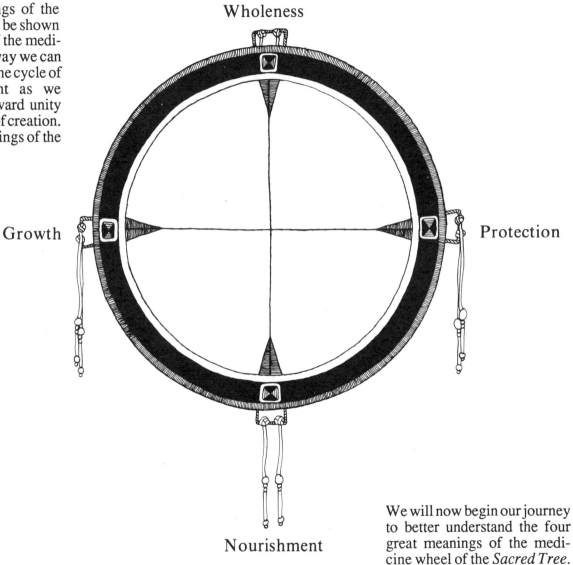

Wholeness

Growth

Protection

Nourishment

We will now begin our journey to better understand the four great meanings of the medicine wheel of the *Sacred Tree*.

23

The Protection of the Sacred Tree

The *Sacred Tree* is a symbol of protection. The shade of the Tree provides protection from the sun. The Tree is also a source of material for our homes and our ceremonial lodges which offer physical and spiritual protection. The Tree provides firewood which gives protection from the cold. The bark of the *Sacred Tree* represents protection from the outside world. The *Sacred Tree* provides the material from which kayaks and canoes are made. The greatest protection of the *Sacred Tree* is to provide a gathering place and central pole of unity for the people.

As a symbol, the *Sacred Tree* represents a safe place for the many tribes and peoples of the world to gather. It provides a place in the world where we can feel secure, a place of peace, a place where we can think, a place where we can feel as one with the Creator. Our mother's womb was a place where we were taken care of and felt safe during the earliest days of life. The *Sacred Tree* can also be thought of as a womb where we can feel safe. It gives birth to our positive life values and to our potential as unique human beings.

The teachings of the *Sacred Tree* help us see a vision, not of what we are, but of what we can become. That vision becomes a path toward our wholeness. So, we see in the protection of the *Sacred Tree* the birth of our wholeness and of our vision of what we can be.

The Nourishment of the Sacred Tree

The second meaning of the *Sacred Tree* is the nourishment it provides to help us live and grow. The symbol for nourishment is the fruit of the Tree. The fruit of the *Sacred Tree* stands for the nourishment a mother gives to her children. It stands for all the care children should receive as they are growing up.

The deeper meaning of the fruit is the nourishment people receive from the world around them. We learn and grow as we relate to other human beings and to the physical and spiritual aspects of the world. The earth is sometimes symbolically called our Mother because it provides for our needs in the same way our mother does.

The leaves of the *Sacred Tree* represent the people. When the leaves of the Tree fall to earth, they will help to nurture the Tree. With their help the Tree can stay healthy, grow and produce flowers and fruit. This is like the passing of our people into the next world. Each generation leaves behind spiritual teachings to help the generation which comes after to live and grow in a healthy way. This symbol of the Tree shows us how important it is to use the wisdom of the past to nourish the present and to plan for the future. This wisdom comes from the hard-won experiences of the countless generations of people who have gone before us. It is taught through the songs, dances, stories, prayers and ceremonies of our people. This wisdom gives us nourishment to develop our full potential.

The leaf is also a symbol of sacrifice. The leaves sacrifice themselves for the future of the *Sacred Tree*. In the same way, the sacrifices in our traditional ceremonies are made on behalf of the life of the tribe and the health of the community. We are taught that our growth during our lives is equal to our service and sacrifice for others. As we serve others, sometimes to the point of sacrifice, we also create more growth in ourselves during our limited time on this earth. Like the leaves of the tree, our efforts to serve others contribute to our own growth.

The Growth of the Sacred Tree

The third meaning of the *Sacred Tree* is growth. The *Sacred Tree* shows us how important it is to search for ences in life which helps us grow and develop. The *Sacred Tree* grows from its central core outward and upward. The inner growth of the Tree is a symbol for the need we all have for an inner life. We grow physically, mentally, emotionally and spiritually as a result of inner work and experiences. We often feel ourselves changing on the inside (in our thoughts and feelings) before we see the changes that later come in our personality and in the way we behave. Others cannot see these changes while they are happening, just as the inner growth of the *Sacred Tree* is hidden. However, we can see the result of this inner growth on the outside of the Tree. Our outer life can be thought of as a reflection of the development of our inner being. We need to deepen and develop the qualities of the four directions within ourselves. As we do, we begin to show these spiritual qualities in our daily lives. This is one of the main teachings of the medicine wheel as it is reflected in the symbol of the *Sacred Tree*.

The *Sacred Tree* teaches us how important it is to have great respect for our inner spiritual growth. The inner growth of the *Sacred Tree* sends forth roots and limbs, which reach out, as if in prayer, to the four directions. Our own inner growth becomes visible in our daily lives through our physical, mental, emotional and spiritual development. We often discover that we are growing as we interact with the world around us. Thus our inner growth becomes visible in our daily lives as our physical, mental, emotional, and spiritual capacities show themselves in how we live.

The growth of the Tree also shows the cycles of time and of life. The changes in the *Sacred Tree* during the four seasons of the year are like the changes we experience in our lives. There are many changes in our lives as we grow and develop in a life-long process of becoming our own true selves. This is an eternal process that reaches beyond life itself. The *Sacred Tree* is rooted in Mother Earth but reaches upward toward a limitless universe. We reach upward toward our potential through struggle and self-determination. If we keep on struggling to heal ourselves and to grow, our efforts are always rewarded by the development of many new and wonderful gifts for ourselves and for our communities.

The Wholeness of the Sacred Tree

The fourth meaning of the *Sacred Tree* is wholeness. We achieve wholeness through unity within ourselves and with others and through the development of the qualities of the four directions. Lamedeer talks about this when he describes the *Sacred Tree* chosen for the sun dance poles:

When the Tree finally arrived in the camp circle, a great shout of joy rose from all the people... The top of the pole was decorated with strips of colored cloth, one each for the four corners of the earth. (Lamedeer)

We learn from the *Sacred Tree* that the Great Spirit is the center pole of creation, a center for balancing and understanding ourselves as human beings. The teachings of the *Sacred Tree* provide a foundation for our lives. On this foundation we can learn what is valuable and important for us. We can find a safe place for developing and protecting all of the different parts of ourselves, both inner and outer. We can reach this balance and understanding because of the teachings of the *Sacred Tree*. Through it we learn that all things in creation work in unity, as one. We achieve unity as we understand and balance the opposite but related qualities of life. The unseen roots in Mother Earth are our inner self which can't be seen. The part of the *Sacred Tree* above ground is that part of us which can be seen. When we understand and balance these parts of ourselves, our Tree will grow rich with fruit that has in it the seeds of further growth, development and wholeness.

We are born into this world with wholeness. Along the path of life we sometimes have experiences that shatter this wholeness. If we have been hurt and somehow broken apart, we need to be made whole again. This can be done through natural healing processes and the spiritual lessons in the teachings of the *Sacred Tree*.

Conclusion

We began by stating that the *Sacred Tree* gives us enough meaning to think about for a lifetime. Here we have been able to briefly touch only the surface of its many meanings. Still, we can at least begin to see how deep these ancient teachings are. We can renew our lives and our oneness with all creation by thinking and acting upon the teachings of the *Sacred Tree*. By doing this we can move toward the wholeness promised by those who have gone before us. It is a time to clean away all the things that are harmful and to build a new life. It is time to gather together under the protection, nourishment, growth and wholeness of the *Sacred Tree*.

IV.   FIRST PRINCIPLES

W hat follows is a summary of some of the important teachings of the *Sacred Tree*. Each one of them is a gate opening onto a path. It is up to the traveller to step through the gate and begin the journey.

1.

Wholeness. All things are interrelated. Everything in the universe is a part of a single whole. Everything is connected in some way to everything else. We can understand something only if we can understand how it is connected to everything else.

28

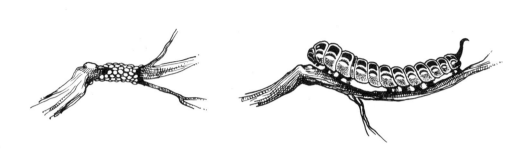

3.

Changes happen in cycles or patterns. They are not accidental or without purpose. Sometimes it is hard to see how a particular change is connected to everything else. This usually means that our ability to see is limited by the situation we are in.

2.

Change. All of creation is constantly changing. Nothing stays the same except the fact that there are always cycles of change. One season follows the other. Human beings are born, live their lives, die and enter the spirit world. All things change. There are two kinds of change. The coming together of things (development) and the coming apart of things (disintegration). Both of these kinds of change are necessary and are always connected to each other.

4.

The seen and the unseen. The physical world is real. The spiritual world is real. Yet, there are separate laws which govern each of them. When we break the spiritual laws, it can affect the physical world. When we break the physical laws, it can affect the spiritual world. A balanced life is one that honors the laws of both the physical world and the spiritual world.

5.

Human beings are spiritual
as well as physical.

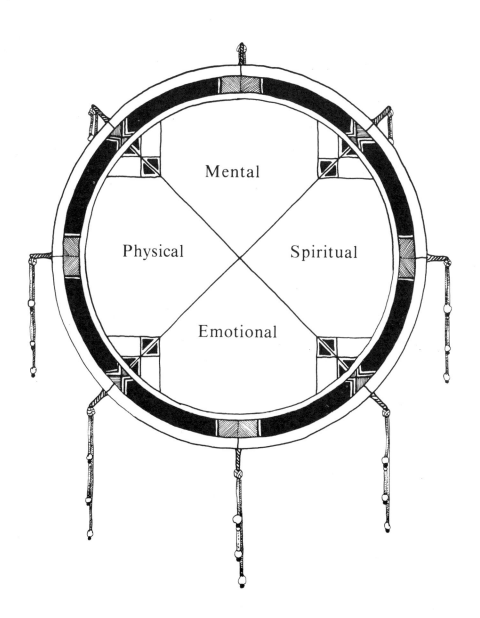

Mental

Physical

Spiritual

Emotional

6.

Human beings can always acquire new gifts, but they must struggle to do so. The timid person may become courageous. The weak person may become bold and strong. The insensitive person may learn to care for the feelings of others. The person who values only money and material things can begin to look inside and listen to his inner voice. When human beings develop new qualities, this process is called "development" or "true learning".

7.

There are four parts of "true learning". These four parts of every person's nature are shown in the four points of the medicine wheel. These four parts of our being are developed through the use of our volition, or will. A person cannot learn in a totally whole and balanced way unless all four parts of her being have been involved in the process.

8.

We develop the spiritual aspect of our nature in four related ways:

First, we have the capacity to respond to non-physical realities like dreams, visions, ideals, spiritual teachings, goals and thoughts.

Second, we have the capacity to understand that these non-physical realities can teach us about our own potential to do or be something more, or different, than we are now.

Third, we have it within us to express these dreams, visions, ideals, spiritual teachings, and our own goals and thoughts by using symbols like language, mathematics and the arts.

Fourth, we have the capacity to use these symbols to guide our future actions. These actions will make it possible for us to "enter into" the vision, or goal we have set before ourselves in the form of symbols, and thus to develop our true potential.

9.

We must become actively involved in the process of developing our own potential.

10.

The doorway through which all must pass if they wish to become more or different than they are now, is the doorway of the will (volition). A person must <u>decide</u> to take the journey. The path has never-ending patience. It will always be there for those who decide to travel it.

11.

Anyone who sets out on a journey of self-development will be helped. There will be guides and teachers who will appear, and spiritual protectors who will watch over the traveller. No test will be given that the traveller does not already have the strength to meet.

12.

The only way to fail on the journey will be our own failure to follow the teachings of the *Sacred Tree*.

V.   THE GIFTS OF THE FOUR DIRECTIONS

Introduction

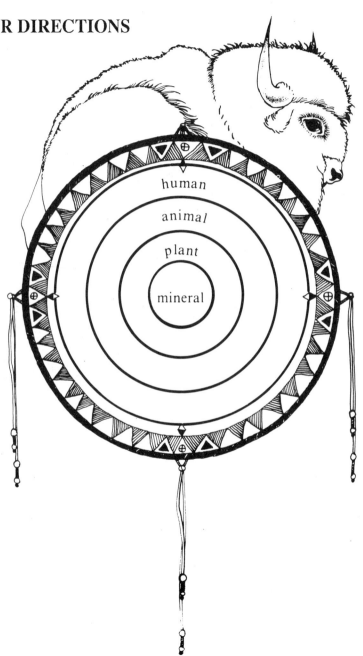

The Medicine Wheel

The medicine wheel is an ancient and powerful symbol of the universe. It is a silent teacher about reality. It shows the many different ways in which all things are connected. It shows things that are and also things that could be.

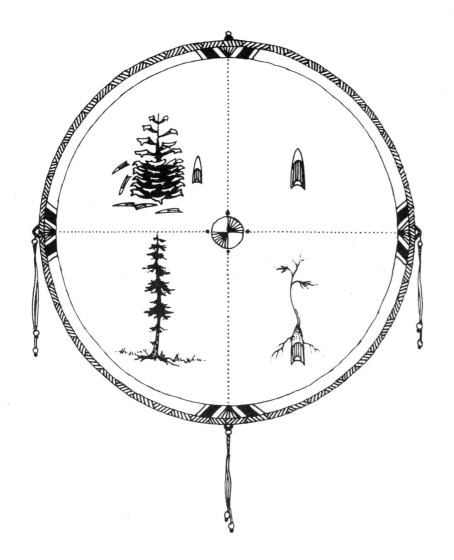

The medicine wheel can be used as a mirror by any sincere person. The medicine wheel not only shows us who we are now, it can also show what we could be if we developed the gifts the Creator has placed within us.

Many of these hidden gifts might never be develop if we do not somehow discover and nurture them. The great spiritual teachers have taught that all the gifts a person has are like the fruits hidden within the Tree.

In one sense, the fruit which has not yet appeared on the tree does not exist. However, in another sense the fruit does exist because the potential to become fruit is there, hidden within the tree. It is a wonderful spiritual power given to human beings by the Creator to be able to see potential as a part of reality and then to be able to decide and act in a way that develops that potential.

The tree can be cut into a thousand pieces and no new fruit will be found, yet when the conditions are right for its growth (warm sunshine, rain, nourishing soil), the Tree will develop the fruit in all of its delicious beauty.

Human beings can create many of the necessary conditions for themselves to develop their own potential. They do this through the operation of their will. They decide to do so.

Unless a person decides and acts in a way that creates the necessary conditions for the development of hidden qualities (such gifts as courage, will-power, clear thinking, or an appreciation of beauty), these gifts remain hidden like the fruit within the young tree.

The medicine wheel can be used as a model of what human beings can become if they decide and act in ways that develop their full potential. Each person who looks deeply into the medicine wheel will see things in a slightly different way. This is because the Creator has made each of us to be a unique human being. We have each been given a special combination of gifts to be used to further develop ourselves and to serve others.

No two people will see exactly the same things when they look deeply into the mirror of the medicine wheel.

Yet everyone who looks deeply will see the tree of their own unique lives with its roots buried deep into the soil of universal truths.

Because many tribes and peoples have used the medicine wheel to look at themselves, there are many different ways of explaining those universal truths that all human beings share.

As we tell about the medicine wheel on the following pages, we have assigned certain gifts to each direction.

We have also chosen certain animals or other aspects of nature to represent qualities or gifts, and lessons.

Some tribes will assign different gifts than we have to each of the points on the circle or to each of the different animals. The teachings telling which qualities make up the complete picture of a human being are nevertheless universal. All tribes teach that human beings have:

1. physical
2. mental
3. emotional
4. spiritual
5. volitional (will)

aspects to their being. All tribes show that the various gifts of the *Sacred Tree* balance one another. Our way of showing this is only one way of showing something that is really universal and could therefore be shown in many ways.

People often use animals as symbols for certain qualities. For example, some have used the eagle to symbolize courage. Others have used the she-bear or the wolverine to symbolize the same thing. We could say that the wolverine is a "teacher" of courage. We say "teacher" because we mean that when we think about the qualities of our brother wolverine, we can learn something about human courage. Many cultures throughout Mother Earth use similar symbols as teachers in their stories and lessons.

The reason different aspects of nature are used as symbols is because many of the human qualities reflected in the medicine wheel are difficult to understand without a living example. By choosing examples from the world around them, people are able to look deeply into the nature of the gift they want to receive. As you use the wheel, you will discover symbols (some animal, some not) that speak deeply and personally to you. It is important that you also feel free to use your own symbols as you discover them.

L et us now take a journey together around the medicine wheel. What you will see, if you look deeply within your own being using the medicine wheel as a mirror, is an image of your strengths and weaknesses, and a vision of what you could become if you were to commit your life to the journey of the medicine wheel. This journey is really the journey of developing your potential as a human being.

We will travel around the wheel as the sun travels around the earth, from the east, to the west.

We will allow each of the directions to represent a certain part of a fully developing person. We cannot say fully *developed* as if it were all over, because human potential never ends. It goes on and on forever.

As you consider the gifts of each of the four directions, you may feel yourself attracted more to some than to others. This may be because of the particular and unique set of gifts the Creator has given especially to you to fulfill your own unique destiny. It may also be because our society emphasizes certain gifts as being somehow better or more desirable than others.

For example, men in many societies are taught that they should be tough, courageous, persevering, and, if need be, hard.

Humility, gentleness, courtesy and a loving heart are considered to be "feminine" qualities and are even laughed at in some groups when these qualities are displayed by a man.

Yet the medicine wheel teaches us that courage must be balanced by wisdom, toughness by gentleness of heart, and not giving up by flexibility. A person who does not achieve this balance in her life will not be able to develop her full potential as a human being. She will not be able to become all that she can be. This is one of the great lessons of the medicine wheel.

As we journey around the wheel, think about your own qualities and gifts. The medicine wheel is a way of measuring your own progress and development. It can also show you what you could work on next in your journey through life.

One final warning is needed. It is dangerous to think of yourself as either a "northern person" or an "eastern person" even though you may feel more attracted to the qualities assigned to one particular direction than to others. In order to use the wheel correctly, you must think of yourself in the center of the wheel, connected equally to all points by the power of your will.

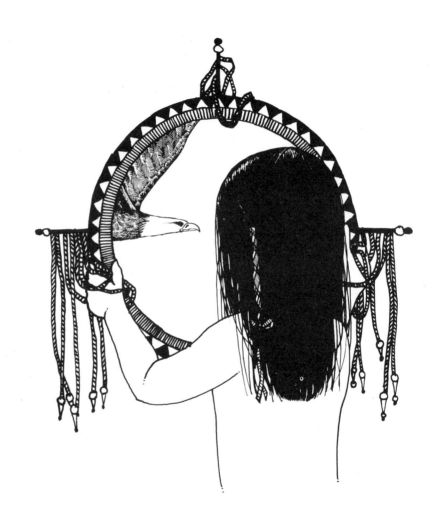

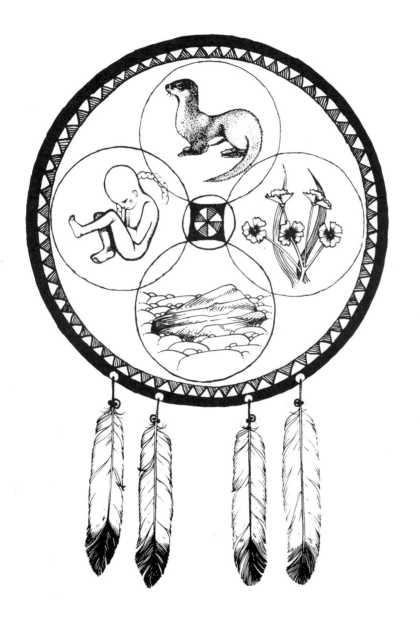

Our journey around the wheel is a symbolic one. What we are really doing is using the patterns found in nature, such as the turning of the seasons, to understand our own selves. We can do this because the universe, in all its splendor and complexity, is reflected within our own beings.

The medicine wheel is a symbolic tool that helps us to see that we are connected with all the rest of creation.

A. The Gifts of the East

The East is the place of all beginnings. The new day comes into the world from the East. It is the direction of renewal and reawakening. It is a place of innocence, and of naturalness, and a place to be happy, joyous and free. It is also the place where we learn to believe in what we cannot yet see.

When we travel to the East, we will be tested with lessons that will teach us many things. There we will learn of warmth of spirit, purity, trust and hope. We will learn how to accept others without criticism. We will learn to love as a child loves; a love that does not question others and does not know itself. Here courage is born and truthfulness begins.

While we are on life's journey, we must return to the East many times. Each time, there will be new things to learn on a new level of understanding.

The East is also the direction from which light comes into the world and where things become clear. Therefore it is the direction of guidance and leadership. It is here that we find the gift of beautiful and clear speech which helps others to understand. We

In the East of the medicine wheel, a good leader learns to see things as they are connected to all other things, to have faith in himself, to have hope for the people and to trust his own vision. But one cannot truly lead the people until a journey is made to the other points of the wheel to learn other lessons. We must travel to the South (the place of the heart), to learn to sacrifice, to be sensitive to others feelings, and

also learn how to see clearly through difficult situations and over a long time. Like the eagle, a leader of the people must often travel alone. The eagle flies high above the world. It watches the movements of all the creatures and knows the hiding place of even the tiniest of them.

How to watch over and guard the well-being of others is an important gift, but one that is difficult to learn. It is one thing to see the situation others are in. It is quite another to care enough about them to want to help. It is yet another to know what to do.

to love and expect nothing in return. We must travel to the West to learn about our unique purpose, about how to use power correctly, and about what the Creator asks of us as leaders. We must travel to the North, to learn how to serve and guide the people with wisdom.

Finally, it will not be until we journey to the far North of the medicine wheel, to the place of wisdom, that we will realize that within everyone of us is hidden the potential to guide others on some part of the journey of the four directions.

45

Learning to Be in the Here and Now

It is in the East of the medicine wheel that all journeys begin. When a path is new, it totally occupies our attention. Our sights are focused on the next few steps. One of the most important gifts to be acquired in the East is the capacity to focus our attention on the events of the present moment. As young children (the East is also the direction of childhood), we instinctively knew how to do this. When we were children and we were busy watching a beautiful butterfly or examining any other interesting new aspect of the world, we were completely absorbed by what we were doing. We had the capacity to be aware of only that butterfly, that patch of ground, or that toy. The animal that many have used to symbolize this capacity is the mouse. Our little mouse sister does what she does with all of her tiny being.

Many people cannot do this. They are always looking to the future, or to the past, or inside or outside, or far away, but seldom to the activity of the present moment. It is this gift of being fully in the present moment that helps us do physical tasks which require that all our senses be alert, and that we give ourselves completely to what we are doing. Some examples of activities that require total attention if the doer is to become truly excellent are hunting, especially in the traditional manner, persons doing crafts such as bead-work, sewing, or woodwork, becoming a healer, play-

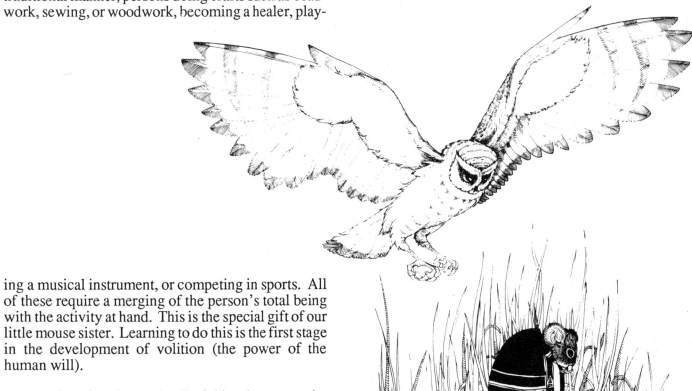

ing a musical instrument, or competing in sports. All of these require a merging of the person's total being with the activity at hand. This is the special gift of our little mouse sister. Learning to do this is the first stage in the development of volition (the power of the human will).

Yet there is a danger in all of this. A person who has learned this quality in the East must also learn to listen to inner warning signs that rumble like thunder

or flash like lightning within us (a lesson of the West). We can become like a mouse who is caught unaware by the hungry owl because she is so absorbed in gathering seeds that she becomes blind to her own danger. We must also be able to look into the future (a lesson of the North) to look at the overall picture (another lesson of the East) in order to ensure our own happiness and well-being.

A person who has never learned the lessons of the South, and is therefore too proud or insensitive to listen to others, or who has never stood in the West of the medicine wheel and seen the fragile little mouse person within himself, may think he's too great to help the people.

It is not an accident that one of the most humble creatures (the mouse) and one of the most noble (the eagle) are the twin teachers of the East, for greatness of spirit and humility are opposite sides of the same reality. The spirit of true leadership is service to the people.

It is only by humbling ourselves to serve others, that we actually become our true selves as human beings. This is the greatest of all the lessons of the medicine wheel. Most people must journey to the East many times in a lifetime to relearn this one lesson.

It would take more than a thousand lifetimes to tell about all of the gifts of the East, or of any of the other direction points on the medicine wheel. The horse that carries the traveller on the journey to search for the gifts of the four directions is named Patience. Without Patience the traveller could not continue the journey. Let us now continue our symbolic journey around the medicine wheel.

B.   The Gifts of the South

The South is the direction of the sun at its highest point. It is the place of summer, of fullness, of physical strength and well-being. It is the place of youth. It is also the time when people work to prepare for the fall and winter months. In this way it is symbolically a place of preparing for the future, of getting ready for the days ahead.

The South is also the place of the heart, of generosity, of sensitivity to the feelings of others, of loyalty, of noble passions and of love.

But the love learned in the South is not the unconditional love for all of creation that a pure-hearted child feels. Nor is it the detached love for the people that our brother, the eagle, in his lonely flight above the world, must learn by journeying to the West.

The love learned in the South is the love of one person for another. How we long to be with the one we love. And how easy it is for this longing to change into a desire to possess and control that person — to have her for ourselves. We can remember this lesson by the symbol of the beautiful rose bush, fragrant, delicate and so inviting to the senses and to the hand. And yet, hidden beneath her soft green leaves are piercing thorns that would tear the flesh of anyone who would seize her beauty and try to own it for herself.

The South direction of the medicine wheel is also the great place of testing for the physical body. There we must learn to discipline our bodies as one would train and discipline a wonderful horse or dog, so that it responds to our every command but never tries to direct our journey.

Many people behave as if they were controlled by their bodies. They cannot separate what their bodies want (certain food or drink, sexual appetite, sleep, etc.) from what is true and good. To exercise this kind of discipline requires determination (an aspect of volition, i.e. the will) to fulfill our purposes and achieve our goals. The ability to choose goals and to decide to go after them is the second stage in the development of the human will.

The senses, such as sight, hearing, touch and taste, are all gifts of the body that can be trained and developed to serve the whole person.

In the South the traveller also gains the gifts of music, gracefulness of movement, appreciation of the arts and the ability to perceive small differences with her eyes, ears and taste buds. One symbol that can be used to represent physical excellence and keen senses is the cougar.

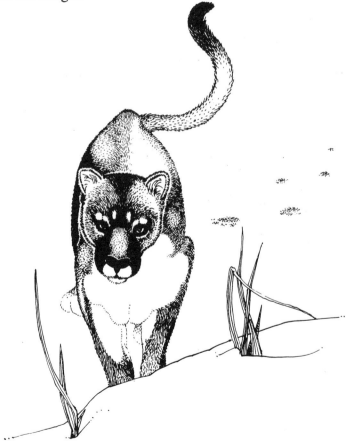

But the cougar is only one of the symbolic teachers of the South. The ability to concentrate, learned in the East from our little mouse sister, becomes, in the South, an intense involvement with the world. In the South, the traveller learns the idealism that makes all great causes possible.

Idealism is a response of the heart to the beauty or ugliness in the world around it. It is not necessarily rooted in deep spiritual insight (a lesson to be learned in the North direction of the medicine wheel). It is really an emotional attraction to what is good or an emotional disgust by what is evil or harmful.

The development of emotional capacities for love, loyalty, generosity, compassion and kindness on the one hand, and our capacity to be angry at injustice and disgusted by senseless violence, are important lessons to be learned in the South.

On the other hand, to hold in feelings of hurt or anger without being able to get rid of them can be very damaging to our physical, emotional, mental and spiritual well-being. There are times when tears of grief run down from Father Sky to Mother Earth so that all of creation might learn to weep. For, until we can understand and get rid of the feelings of anger, resentment and hurt that we have taken inside of us, these feelings will continue to block our intelligence and chill our capacity for genuine love and warmth. This is true for many of our people at this time.

The most difficult and valuable gift to look for in the South of the medicine wheel is the capacity to express feelings openly and freely in ways that do not hurt other beings.

The practical value of this is that we will then have the ability to set aside our feelings of anger, hurt, or grief so that we can listen to, or in other ways help, those around us. We will also be able to release, in a good way, our own feelings of hurt that prevent us from being clear-thinking and effective human beings.

Our feelings (such as anger, fear, or love) do not "happen" to us like a rock dropped on our heads. The popular phrase "falling in love" shows that many people believe that love happens to them. Yet wise teachers and elders know that feelings can be realized and controlled by an act of our will. Indeed, feelings can be made clearer, evaluated and developed.

We can discipline our feelings just like we can train and develop our body through the exercise of the will. For example, people who fly into uncontrollable anger because they have not been given something they want, have not learned to discipline the powers of emotion. People who are so overcome with excitement or fear in an emergency that they are unable to act to help themselves or others, also have not learned to discipline their feelings.

A symbol of this important lesson is the red willow tree, the other great teacher of the South. The red willow is both the strongest and the most flexible in the forest. It can survive flood, fire, severe winter, and droughts. It yields to forces that would destroy the other trees, but it always springs back. The lesson of our sister, the willow, can always be remembered by the beautiful music of the whistles and flutes that we make from her branches.

Let us now continue our symbolic journey around the medicine wheel, for there is still much to learn.

54

C. The Gifts of the West

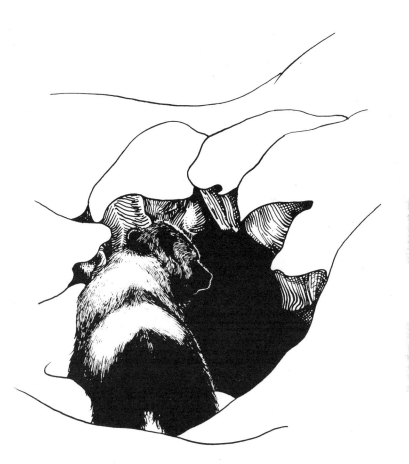

The West is the direction from which darkness comes. It is the direction of the unknown, of going within, of dreams, of prayer and of meditation. The West is the place of testing, where the will is stretched to its outer limits so that the gift of perseverance may be won. Perseverance means to continue to do something even though it may be hard.

For the nearer we get to a goal, the more difficult the journey becomes. The capacity to stick to a challenge even though it is very hard and even painful is an important lesson to be learned in the West. It is the third great lesson in the development of our will.

Because thunder and lightning often come from there, the West is also the direction (symbolically) of power. In many traditions, the West is where the Thunder Beings live. These are the bringers of power. Power to heal. Power to protect and defend. Power to see and to know. Here the traveller must learn to manage power in ways that are in harmony with the great universal teachings of the *Sacred Tree*.

Two teachers of the West (symbolically) are the black bear and the turtle. A person who has travelled to the West and received the gifts that wait for her there will, like the black bear, have great strengths. But the source of that strength will come from deep within the person. Like the bear who retires to a dark, private place in the face of winter coldness, a person who has learned the lessons of the West balances the intense loyalty of the South with deep spiritual insight. This insight is gained by shutting out the noise of the world, and by going alone to pray and be tested.

One of the guides on this inner journey can be pictured (symbolically) as the turtle. The turtle not only teaches to go within, but also grants the gift of perseverance (continuing to do something even though it may be hard) to those who learn his ways.

By journeying to the center of our beings, it is possible for us to experience the connection between the human spirit and the rest of the universe. It is also possible for us to experience the connection between the human spirit and the Creator. This experience is the gift of prayer.

To enter the place of learning and testing deep within us requires a great daily effort. Each morning when we get up, and each night before going to sleep, the elders have taught us that we must meet our Creator alone. One way to do this is to set aside a room in our house, or a part of a room, or some other special place, and to use that place every day for prayer, meditation and deep personal reflection.

Sacred Objects

Many people collect objects on their journey that are special to them. For some it may be a certain book or photograph. For others, it may be things from nature such as a feather, a small stone, or some special herb. These things usually symbolize, to the holder, parts of that person's spiritual journey through life. If we understand how to use these objects, they can help us become aware of how ordinary everyday things can have great meaning in our spiritual life.

When people understand that it is not the objects themselves that are the source of power, but rather the deep meaning these objects have to the person who uses them, then the use of sacred objects can greatly help a person to focus themselves in preparation for prayer and meditation.

No Time for Inner Life

We must find time in our lives to pray and to meditate. We must make time to reflect deeply on why we have been created and what we must do with our lives. We must make time to listen with all of our being to the guidance of the universe. If we don't, then we are like a bird who has not yet learned to fly. All the parts of the bird are present, but something is still missing. To be a whole person is to be alive in a physical, emotional, mental and spiritual way.

Signs of Spiritual Emptiness

A sign that much work is needed in the area of personal spiritual growth is when a person dislikes being alone, especially in silence. Many people use television or recorded music to fill the silence so that they do not have to experience themselves as they really are.

To face ourselves alone in silence, and to love ourselves because the Creator has made us beautiful, are things that every developing human being needs to learn. From this position of strength, no one can put us down, and no one can lead us to do or to be anything else but what we know we must do or be.

Another sign that warns the traveller that her heart is empty of the gifts of the West is when she does not feel respect for the elders, or for the spiritual activities and struggles of other people. To laugh and ridicule spiritual things is to say: I feel an emptiness within me that I must hide by my criticism of others or by my pretended laughter.

The Greatest Lesson Of the West

The greatest lesson to be learned from the symbolic teachers of the West is to accept ourselves as we really are as both spiritual and physical beings and to never again cut ourselves off from the spiritual part of our nature.

The West is the place of sacrifice. When we stand in the West we learn that nothing may be taken from the universe unless something is given. For each of the great gifts of the medicine wheel there is a price. And yet we will learn that the mystery of sacrifice is that there is no sacrifice.

From the West we can look over to the East, to the place of innocence and first beginnings. There we can see ourselves standing naked to the universe, vulnerable and small before the stars. It is only when we can see ourselves in that way that we receive the gift of humility.

And we can look over to the South and there we can see ourselves struggling to discipline our bodies and to purify our feelings. We see the pain of love in our eyes and the heat of conviction in our faces, and we realize that these things are good. But that they are only touch points on a very long journey, and then we receive the gift of spiritual insight.

For when we look at our lives in a spiritual way, we come to understand why it is that we have been sent to the world by the Creator.

When, in our symbolic journey to the West, we receive the gifts of prayer and meditation, we will come (though never complete) to know, and then to love the Creator. This love will be so intense that the heat of that love will become a flame that devours all other love — much like the moth is devoured by the flame of the candle from which it is so unable to stay away from. Then we will know that somehow this love fulfills one of the great purposes for which we have been created.

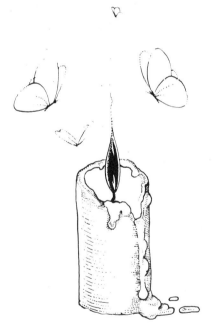

As we look from our watching place in the West and see ourselves struggling to learn the discipline of the South, we will realize that the journey to the four

directions to receive the gifts and lessons of each of them fulfills another of the Creator's great purposes. We realize that all human beings should struggle (little by little, day by day) to develop themselves as much as possible.

And then we will look over to the eastern horizons where our brother, the eagle, soars. We will see him there, ready to serve the people, and ready to do all he can to help them make the journey of the medicine wheel together. In this way their civilization can develop and flourish. Then we will realize that what he does, we must all do in our own way. For such is the purpose of the Creator.

There are many other gifts the traveller can discover in the West, such as the gift of fasting, the gift of ceremony, the gift of clear self-knowledge, and the gift of vision. All are important, but the gift of vision is especially important.

It is important to see clearly, with our inner eye, what we can become if we take the necessary journey. This clear vision is as necessary to human development as rain and sunshine are necessary to the growth of plants. This is because human beings develop and grow through their own decisions. We must have some vision, some ideal or goal to look toward, or else we will have no way of knowing what we must do. It is also very important that our vision be a true one. Many people believe that they are much less than what they could be. Because they cannot see any other possibility for themselves than their present undeveloped condition, they stop struggling, and give up their symbolic journey around the medicine wheel.

In the youthfulness of the South, the heart is drawn to goals and ideals, but these may, or may not, be good goals or good ideals.

The inner spiritual vision learned from the symbolic teachers of the West help us to judge our ideals, goals and actions against a spiritual understanding about what a human being really is, and about how human beings grow and develop.

63

D.   The Gifts of the North

T he North is the place of winter, of white snows that remind us of the white hair of our elders. It is the dawning place of true wisdom. Here live the teachers of intellectual gifts. They can be symbolized by the great mountain and the sacred lake. Some of the special gifts that wait for the traveller in the North of the medicine wheel include the following capacities.

to think
to synthesize
to speculate
to predict
to discriminate
to solve problems
to imagine
to analyze
to understand
to calculate
to organize
to criticize
to remember
to interpret hidden meanings

There is much we can do to develop these gifts. The very first step is to realize that we can all possess them. The way that they can be obtained, however, and even the way they will show themselves, will be slightly different for each person.

The body of a great runner can be disciplined until it has learned tremendous endurance and great speed. In the same way, the mind can be trained until it becomes a highly developed instrument.

When the warrior begins training, he is nearly overwhelmed by how difficult it is to run long distances or to go without food for many days. Travellers who wish to acquire the gifts of the North will also often feel (at the beginning) that the task is too great or that they do not have the necessary capacity to learn.

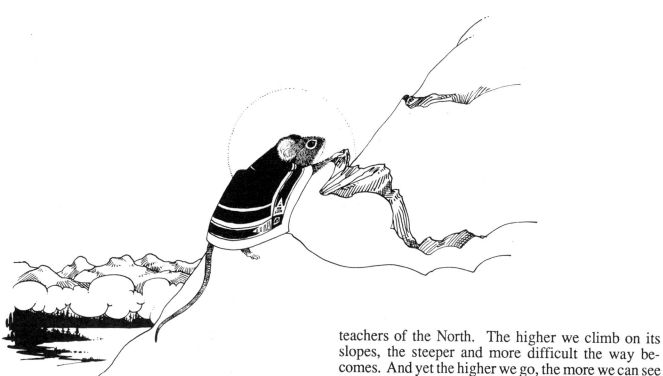

teachers of the North. The higher we climb on its slopes, the steeper and more difficult the way becomes. And yet the higher we go, the more we can see and the stronger we can become.

Let us take one gift, the gift of memory, and think about its development. We are not born with "poor memories." We are born with the capacity to learn and remember four or five languages at a time, or to be able to repeat exactly what we have seen and heard even if it is very complicated. One proof of this is that by the age of three or four years, you already knew nearly the entire language spoken in your community. Had you been born in China, you would have spoken Chinese just as easily as you now speak your own language. But over the years you have, for many reasons, stopped using that tremendous capacity to remember things that you were given by the Creator.

One of the great lessons of the medicine wheel is that all human beings can acquire gifts in all of the directions. However, many of the gifts do not come automatically, or even easily. Often a decision is required, along with a great deal of daily effort over a long period of time. The great mountain is one of the

If you had not stopped, you would be able, whenever you wanted, at will, to repeat back the details of almost everything that you have ever heard, read, or thought about in school or in your life. It is possible to learn how to do this. It is possible, through special training, to develop a memory so keen that you would be considered a genius wherever you went. It is possible, for example, to glance at 30 or 50 objects on a table or in a room, and then hours or even days later, be able to repeat exactly the name and location of each object.

This and many other capacities of the mind are the birthright of every human being. We have only to journey to the North, and there to struggle. For nothing is gained without a price.

Completion

The North can also be seen as the direction of completion and fulfillment. Here the traveller learns the lessons of all things that end.

Here the powers of volition reach their highest point as we learn to complete what began as a far away vision. The capacity to finish what we have started is of very great importance to our well-being. This is the final lesson in the development of the powers of volition (the will).

We have learned from the teachers who live in the West, that the closer one gets to finishing of a goal, the more difficult the journey becomes. To help us in our life's struggles, the Creator has given the gift of perseverance (the ability to stick to a difficult task). But even with perseverance we hesitate in the end when we are not sure that the goal is near and that it can indeed be won.

Detachment

We must have the knowledge and wisdom to judge whether or not the time of completion is really near. These are gained through the door of detachment. The gift of detachment gives the traveller the ability to see as one the past, the present and the future.

Detachment means freedom from hate, jealousy, desire anger and fear. It means completely letting go of all things, even those which we love the best. It means being able to put behind us all the knowledge we have gained on our journeys. Knowledge itself can be a burden too heavy to carry to the top of the great mountain and to the shores of the sacred lake.

To let go of something (like knowledge or love or hate) is not to throw it away. It is to step outside its shadow so that things can be seen in a different light.

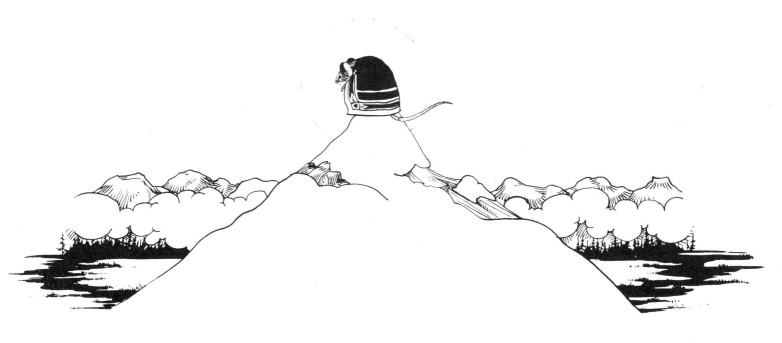

It is difficult, but very important, to learn how to stand apart from the things we believe to be true, or from our fears, our anger, our jealousy, our hate, or even from our love for someone. All of these can control us and stop us from thinking clearly.

Fear, anger, jealousy, and hate can completely cloud a person's intelligence. Wise teachers tell us to stay away from these just like we would stay away from a poisonous snake. If love is not balanced by reason, it can also prevent a person from seeing clearly.

In order to stand apart from our strong feelings and thoughts, we must learn to look at ourselves from the center of the medicine wheel. From that center, we will be able to see how we fit together with everything else. We will see ourselves as a small but truly sacred part of a very large process.

When we live in that balanced center point, we cannot be controlled by our strong feelings or thoughts. From this sacred center, whatever action we take will be taken because we decided to act, and because it was good to do so.

69

When we can look at ourselves in this way, we will have learned the first lesson in detachment: We will have learned that we are not our bodies, we are not our thoughts, we are not our feelings or our insights. We are something else far deeper and wider. We are the being that has thoughts, and insights. We are the being that feels and knows. We can watch our feelings, our thoughts, and our insights and know that they are reflections in the mirror of the sacred lake.

When we have truly mastered detachment we will understand the mystery of surrender. We will be able to put ourselves completely in the hands of the Creator, moment by moment, we will understand that everything that comes to us in our lives is to help us to grow and develop spiritually. We will understand that we cannot be a good leader until we have been in front of the most fierce battles and have had our inner being tested in every way. Then we will be able to express unconditional love and faith at all times and under all conditions.

The beginning of detachment and the beginning of surrender is learned in the fires of love. The end of detachment is learned in quiet moments on the silent shores of the sacred lake, and cannot be told.

The Final Gift

It is possible for the traveller to be so greatly in love with the gifts of any one of the directions that he may forget the journey and attempt to live forever with the teachers that have so captured his heart.

For example, a person may come to believe that if he has received the great intellectual gifts of the North, he does not need to keep learning. It is very dangerous for the traveller to try to live forever in any one of the directions. Our true home is in the center of the universe, and it is to the center that we must always return.

If a person gives up the journey because he feels he has found all that he needs in the gifts of one of the directions, great harm can come to him. For he will have shut himself off from a big part of his own true self. He will also have created an imbalance that could seriously harm him.

A person who wants to stay in the North, shutting out the gifts of the other directions, will be caught in an icy coldness, like that of winter. He will be cut off from the warmth of his own heart.

Indeed, each of the gifts of each of the directions is balanced by other gifts. The boldness of the eagle is balanced by the humility of the willow and the careful wisdom of the turtle. The idealism of the South is balanced by the wisdom and clarity of thought learned in the North.

The final lesson of the North is the lesson of balance, for wisdom teaches how all things fit together. And balance, when it is applied to the connection between all human beings, becomes justice. Justice is the greatest gift of the North. With its aid, the traveller can see all things as they really are. Without it, there can be no peace or security in the affairs of the world.

When we stand in the North, we can look over to the South and see ourselves singing the tender songs of love. We realize that to know and understand is not only a thing of the head, but also of the heart. We can look to the East and there see the beautiful joy of our little mouse sister as she gazes at the western horizon, to the place of things unknown. We see her wonderful ability to believe even though she cannot see. Then we realize that there is much more to be known than all the knowledge that all the wisest elders have ever known, and we are humbled.

The mystery of all endings is found in the birth of new beginnings. There is no ending to the journey of the four directions. The human capacity to develop never stops. The medicine wheel turns forever.

Summary Chart
The Gifts of the Four Directions

East

- light
- beginning
- renewal
- innocence
- guilelessness
- spontaneity
- joy
- capacity to believe in the unseen
- warmth of spirit
- purity
- trust
- hope
- uncritical acceptance of others
- love that doesn't question others and doesn't know itself
- courage
- truthfulness
- birth
- rebirth
- childhood
- illumination
- guidance
- leadership
- beautiful speech
- vulnerability
- ability to see clearly through complex situations
- watching over others
- guiding others
- seeing situations in perspective
- hope for the people
- trust in your own vision
- ability to focus attention on present time tasks
- concentration
- devotion to the service of others

South

- youth
- fullness
- summer
- the heart
- generosity
- sensitivity to the feelings of others
- loyalty
- noble passions
- love (of one person for another)
- balanced development of the physical body
- physical discipline
- control of appetites
- determination
- goal setting
- training senses such as sight, hearing, taste
- musical development
- gracefulness
- appreciation of the arts
- discrimination in sight hearing and taste
- passionate involvement in the world
- idealism
- emotional attraction to good and repulsion to bad
- compassion
- kindness
- anger at injustice
- repulsion by senseless violence
- feelings refined, developed, controlled
- ability to express hurt and other bad feelings
- ability to express joy and good feelings
- ability to set aside strong feelings in order to serve others

West

- darkness
- the unknown
- going within
- dreams
- deep inner thoughts
- testing of the will
- perseverance
- stick-to-it-iveness
- consolidation of personal power
- management of power
- spiritual insight
- daily prayer
- meditation
- fasting
- reflection
- contemplation
- silence
- being alone with one's self
- respect for elders
- respect for others' beliefs
- respect for the spiritual struggles of others
- sacrifice
- awareness of our spiritual nature
- humility
- love for the Creator
- commitment to the path of personal development
- commitment to universal life values and a high moral code
- commitment to struggle to assist the development of the people
- ceremony
- clear self-knowledge
- vision (a sense of possibilities and potentialities)

North

- elders
- wisdom
- thinking
- analyzing
- understanding
- speculating
- calculation
- prediction
- organizing
- categorizing
- discriminating
- criticizing
- problem solving
- imagining
- interpreting
- integrating all intellectual capacities
- completion
- fulfillment
- lessons of things that end
- capacity to finish what we begin
- detachment
- surrender to the will of the Creator
- freedom from fear
- freedom from hate
- freedom from love
- freedom from knowledge
- seeing how all things fit together
- insight
- intuition made conscious
- sense of how to live a balanced life
- capacity to dwell in the center of things, to see and take the middle way
- moderation
- justice

VI. CODE OF ETHICS

Besides the sacred teachings about the nature of life, and about the gifts of the four directions, the teachings of the *Sacred Tree* also include a code of ethics. This code of ethics will help us find happiness and well-being if we live our lives according to its teachings. It describes what wisdom means in the relationship between individuals, in family life, and in the life of the community. These are the sparkling gems of experience practiced by people on the sacred path everywhere. They represent the safe path which leads around the medicine wheel, and up the great mountain to the sacred lake. What follows is a summary of some of the most important of these teachings that are universal to all tribes.

1.

Each morning when you wake up, and each evening before sleeping, give thanks for the life within you, for all life, for the good things the Creator has given you and others, and for the opportunity to grow a little more each day. Give thanks for yesterday's thoughts and actions and for the courage and strength to be a better person. Ask for the things that will benefit everyone.

2.

Respect. Respect means "to feel or show honour or esteem for someone or something; to consider the well-being of, or to treat someone or something with deference or courtesy." Showing respect is a basic law of life.

- Treat every person, from the tiniest child to the oldest elder with respect at all times.
- Special respect should be given to elders, parents, teachers and community leaders.
- Don't make anyone feel "put down" by you; avoid hurting other hearts as you would avoid a deadly poison.
- Don't touch anything that belongs to someone else (especially sacred objects) without permission, or an understanding between you.
- Speak in a soft voice, especially when you are with elders, strangers or others who should be especially respected.
- Never interrupt people who are having a conversation.

- Respect the privacy of every person. Never interfere with a person's quiet moments or personal space
- Never walk between people who are having a conversation.
- Do not speak unless you are invited to do so at gatherings where elders are present (except to ask what is expected of you when you aren't quite sure).
- Never speak about others in a negative ways, whether they are present or not.
- Treat the earth and all of her aspects as your mother. Show deep respect for the mineral world, the plant world, and the animal world. Do nothing to pollute the air or the soil. If others want to destroy our mother, rise up with wisdom to defend her.
- Show deep respect for the beliefs and religions of others.
- Listen with courtesy to what others say, even if you feel that what they are saying is worthless.
- Listen with your heart.

3.

Respect the wisdom of the people in council. Once you give an idea to a council or a meeting, it no longer belongs to you. It belongs to the people. Respect demands that you listen carefully to the ideas of other people in council, and that you do not insist that your idea is the best. You should freely support the ideas of others if they are true and good, even if those ideas are quite different from the ones you have contributed. The clash of ideas brings forth the spark of truth.

Once a council has decided something in unity, respect demands that no one speak secretly against what has been decided. If the council has made an error, that error will become clear to everyone in its own time.

4.

Be truthful at all times, and under all conditions.

5.

Aways treat your guests with honour and consideration. Give your best food, your best blankets, the best part of your house, and your best service to your guests.

6.

The hurt of one is the hurt of all, the honour of one is the honour of all.

7.

Receive strangers and outsiders with a loving heart and as members of the human family.

8.

All the races and tribes in the world are like the different coloured flowers of one meadow. All are beautiful. As children of the Creator they must all be respected.

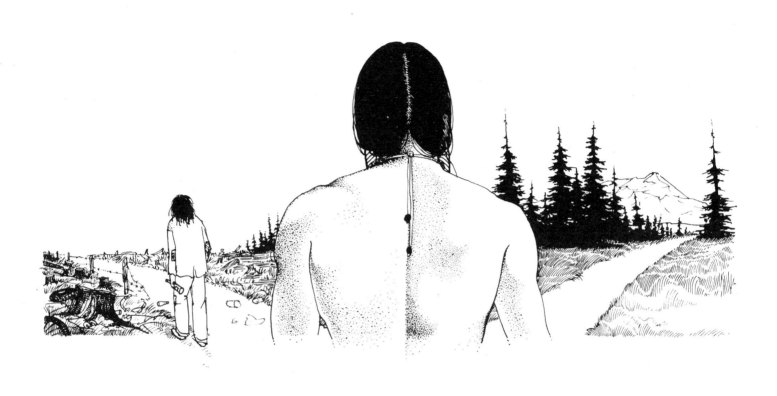

9.

To serve others, to be of some use to family, community, nation or the world is one of the main purposes for which human beings have been created. Do not fill yourself with your own affairs and forget your most important task. True happiness comes only to those who dedicate their lives to the service of others.

10.

Observe moderation and balance in all things.

11.

Know those things that lead to your well-being and those things that lead to your destruction.

12.

Listen to and follow the guidance given to your heart. Expect guidance to come in many forms: in prayer, in dreams, in times of quiet aloneness and in the words and deeds of wise elders and friends.

Conclusion

Gaining an understanding of the *Sacred Tree* is a never-ending journey. As in all journeys, there must be time for activity, as well as for rest.

It is our deep prayer that the Great Spirit will bless and guide your every step on this journey into an ever greater vision of beauty, truth, love, wisdom and justice, and that you will join us again in search of a greater understanding of the *Sacred Tree*.

To be continued . . .